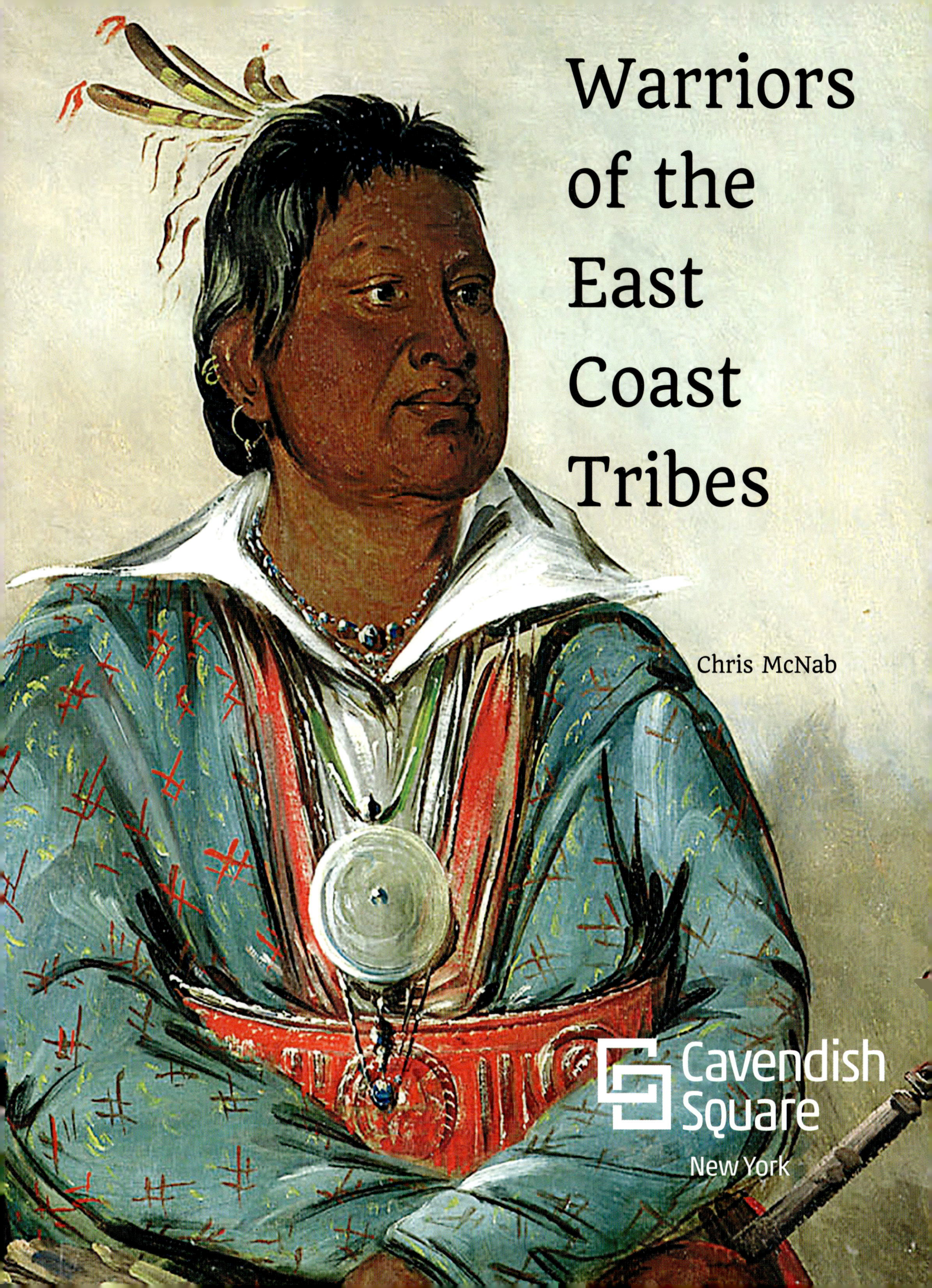

Warriors of the East Coast Tribes

Chris McNab

Cavendish Square
New York

This edition published in 2018 by Cavendish Square Publishing, LLC
243 5th Avenue, Suite 136, New York, NY 10016

First Edition

Cataloging-in-Publication Data

Names: McNab, Chris.
Title: Warriors of the east coast tribes / Chris McNab.
Description: New York : Cavendish Square, 2018. | Series: Native American warfare | Includes bibliographical references and index. | Audience: Grades 6–10.
Identifiers: ISBN 9781502632845 (library bound) | ISBN 9781502633125 (ebook)
Subjects: LCSH: Indians of North America—Canada, Eastern—Juvenile literature. | Indians of North America--East (U.S.)—Juvenile literature. | Indians of North America—Wars—Juvenile literature.
Classification: LCC E78.E2 M259 2018 | DDC 970.004'97—dc23

Editorial Director: David McNamara
Associate Art Director: Amy Greenan
Production Coordinator: Karol Szymczuk

The photographs in this book are used by permission and through the courtesy of: All maps and black-and-white line artworks produced by JB Illustrations © Amber Books; AKG Images: 47 & 75 (North Wind Picture Archives), 162 (North Wind Picture Archives); Alamy: 98tr (North Wind Picture Archives); Art Archive: 128/129 (William E. Weiss/Buffalo Bill Historical Center), 194 (Buffalo Bill Historical Center); Bridgeman Art Library: 88/89 (Peter Newark American Pictures), 104/105bl (Peter Newark American Pictures), 120 (Look & Learn), 133 (Peter Newark American Pictures), 135 & 151 (Look & Learn), 174 & 197 (Peter Newark American Pictures); Corbis: 19 & 20 (Bettmann), 22t (Werner Forman Archive), 32 (Robert Wagenhoffer), 39 (Marilyn Angel Wynn/Nativestock Pictures), 42, 55 (Medford Historical Society Collection), 56/57 (Historical Picture Archive), 58 (Historical Picture Archive), 62 (Nik Wheeler), 63, 64, 83 (Bettmann), 86 (Peter Harholdt), 112, 137, 143, 146, 152, 157, 158, 159, 160 (Bettmann), 161 (Poodles Rock), 165tr, 165b (Tria Giovan), 176, 184 (Bettmann), 192 (Werner Forman Archive), 206, 209, 210, 211, 214/215 (Bettmann) Dorling Kindersley: 105t (Geoff Brightling) Getty Images: 8 (Bridgeman Art Library), 11 (Roger Viollet), 15 (Joe Sohm/Visions of America), 25 (Time & Life Pictures), 29 (Marilyn Angel Wynn/Nativestock Pictures), 36, 48 & 74 (Bridgeman Art Library), 78br (Science & Society Picture Library), 79tr & 97 (Hulton Archive), 140 & 145 (Time & Life Pictures), 148 (SuperStock), 150 (Bridgeman Art Library), 170/171 (Hulton Archive), 177 (Hulton Archive), 178 (Marilyn Angel Wynn/Nativestock Pictures), 193 (Bridgeman Art Library), 204/205, 207 (Hulton Archive); iStockphoto: 153 (Duncan Walker); Library of Congress: 9, 12/13, 17, 27tr, 41, 45, 49, 50/51, 54, 59, 65tl, 65b, 70, 72tr, 76, 85tl, 85br, 98bl, 100, 106, 109tl, 111, 115, 117, 118, 119, 121, 125, 127tr, 130, 139, 141 (both), 144, 154/155, 156, 163, 164, 167, 168 & 169 (all), 180 (both), 183 & 183 (both), 185, 187, 188, 195, 198/199, 200, 208; Mary Evans Picture Library: 81, 147, 181; Photos.com: 78/79tl, 90, 91, 109b, 127b, 172, 175; Photoshot: 6/7 (World Illustrated), 22bl & 113 (UPPA), 179 (UPPA); Public Domain: 72bl, 122; TopFoto: 102/103 (Granger Collection), 138 & 191 (Granger Collection); U.S. Department of Defense: 213; Werner Forman Archive: 27b (Ohio State Museum), 202 (Anthropological Museum of Lomonosov, Moscow).

Printed in the United States of America

CONTENTS

Introduction

The tribes of eastern North America occupied a vast swathe of territory, running from the subarctic shores of Canada down to the tropical swamplands of Florida. Although this chapter incorporates the whole eastern slice of North America, in terms of the Native American tribes living there, historians have traditionally divided the territory into two cultural portions—Northeast and Southeast—while also bracketing many of the Eastern tribes as "Woodlands Indians."

The "Woodlands"' definition is useful, because it alludes to the fact that the society, warmaking, and culture of the Eastern Native American tribes was largely defined by the extremely fertile terrain that dominates the eastern United States and Canada. The Southeast culture area, reaching from the Gulf of Mexico up to the Midwest and out to mid-Texas, was geophysically defined by marshland (saltwater and freshwater), swamps, floodplains (particularly along the mighty Mississippi River), grasslands and the fertile mountains of the southern Appalachians. The Northeast culture area, running from southeastern Canada down to Maryland and Virginia, by contrast, was dominated by major river and broadleaf and coniferous forest systems, with elevated land provided by the northern Appalachians. The Great Lakes, and the river systems of the region, provided fishing and trade.

The nature of the terrain in eastern North America was critical in dictating the tactics, weaponry and strategies of the Eastern Native American tribes. As we shall see, in such environments, stealth, ambush and raiding tactics were at a premium, with the Native Americans essentially practicing "irregular warfare" against the largely conventional tactics of the European settlers.

◀ The battle of Tippecanoe, November 7, 1811. The warriors of Shawnee chief Tecumseh were pitted against a 1000-strong settler force under General William Henry Harrison. Although the Indians launched a stealthy opening attack, they were finally undone by a mass bayonet charge by the militia, a tactic the Indians were unused to facing.

CHAPTER 1

North and South

This study will begin by examining the tribes who inhabited the east, and how they related to one another and to the settlers who colonized their lands. Taking the Northeast area first, the tribes of this territory are often broadly categorized according to their language group— Algonquian-speaking and Iroquois-speaking, although there were some tribes that fell outside of this neat division.

The Iroquois

The Iroquois are particularly interesting for our study, because when they perceived a threat from rival tribes in the late 1500s, they formed a powerful confederacy from the union of five tribes—the Seneca, Oneida, Mohawk, Cayuga and Onondaga—with the Tuscarora tribe of North Carolina later joining the Confederacy in the early 1700s (see map below).

IROQUOIS FIVE NATIONS TERRITORY 1650

The map here shows the boundaries of the Five Nations of Iroquois in 1650, while the arrows indicate the routes of expansion the tribes took before being curtailed by settler outgrowth. The Iroquois Confederacy was one of the most substantial of the Native American alliances, and it benefited as much from intelligent associations with the colonists as from alliances with one another. The Confederacy was shattered at the end of the eighteenth century, when the Iroquois backing of the British in the American Revolution consigned them to the losing side in the war.

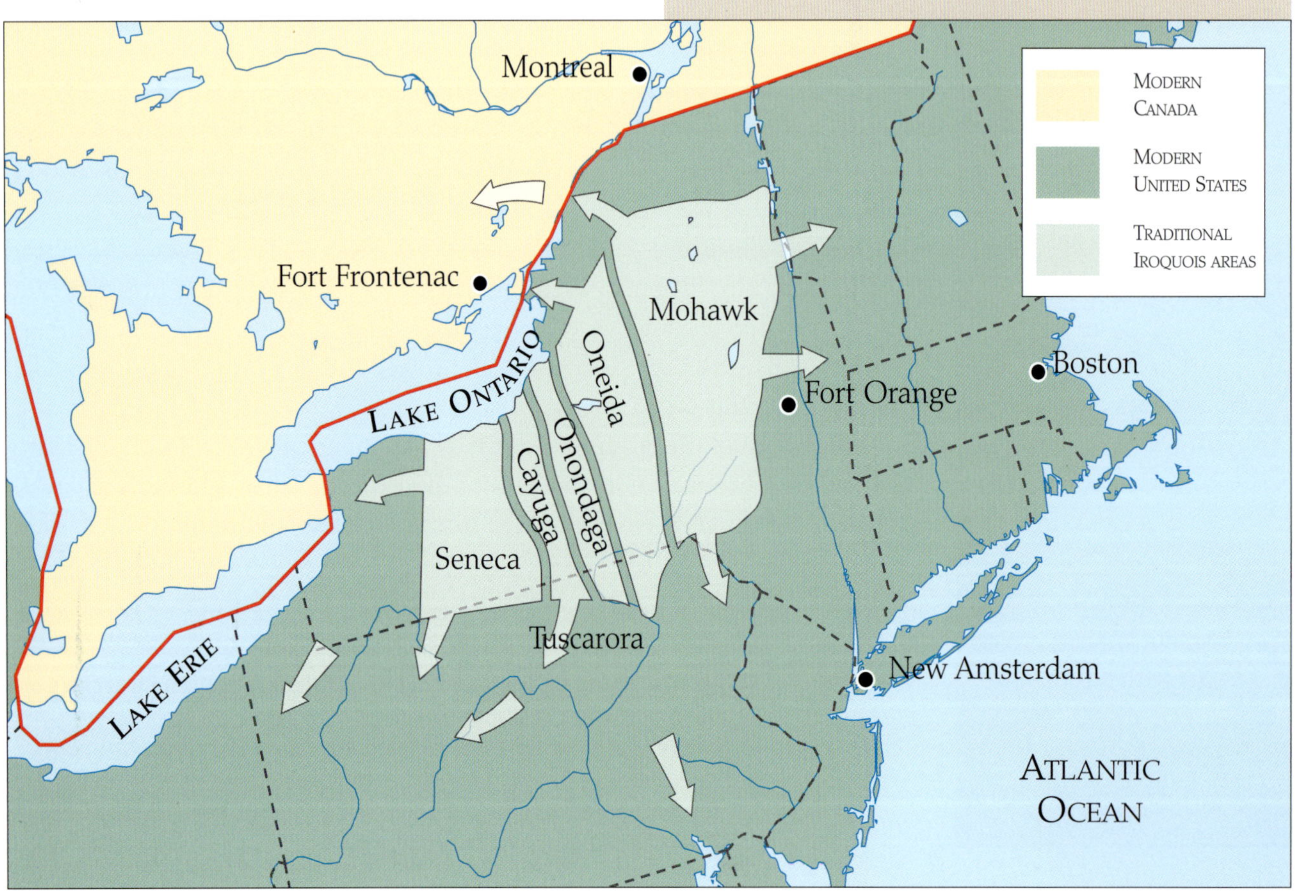

▲ **The northeastern American landscape provided the perfect terrain for Eastern Indian-style warfare. Lakes, rivers and forest trails provided routes of travel, while woodlands gave numerous sites for ambushes.**

The Iroquois Confederacy was one of the most powerful unified bodies of Native Americans in the whole of North America. Although the confederate structure did not interfere in the individual management of tribal affairs, except in dispute mediation, a 50-member council drawn from all the tribes acted as a kind of "foreign office" for looking after the Confederacy's interests. The Iroquois increased their power through a close trading relationship with the Dutch and then the British from the early 1600s, associations that brought them imported European firearms. But relations with the French were far less amicable, particularly once French forces allied themselves with the rival Huron tribe in a military campaign against the Iroquois in the Saint Lawrence Valley (see Chapter 2).

The Iroquois' enmity towards the French resulted in frequent attacks on French settlements and an alliance with the British during the French and Indian War (1754–63). The alliance with the British brought the Royal Proclamation of 1763, in which the British guaranteed that all land west of the Appalachians would remain in the hands of the Native Americans. Iroquois territory, centred in the 1600s to the east and south of Lake Ontario, subsequently expanded south down the Allegheny, Susquehanna and Delaware rivers, east across the Hudson River and west towards Lake Huron. The Iroquois appeared to be in the ascendant.

Yet history had other ideas. Despite four of the six Iroquois nations allying themselves with the British during the American Revolution (1775–83), the British lost their rebellious colony and the Iroquois equally lost significant portions of their land, with many of their peoples heading north into Canada. Those that remained were progressively driven out by an American expansion during the first half of the nineteenth century.

THE FRENCH AND INDIAN WAR (1754–63)

This war was principally a war between colonizers—the British and the French—but it inevitably sucked in the Native

Iroquois Loyalist
An Iroquois warrior shows typical dress for the eighteenth century. Armed with a flintlock "trade gun," he wears a fabric smock, buckskin leggings (tied with garters to reduce snagging when moving through undergrowth) and has a shaven head decorated with a simple feathered headdress.

Americans of the affected territories. The conflict was sparked by the friction between the British and the French in eastern Canada and what would become the northeastern United States. British expansion into Pennsylvania, New York and Ohio Country in the mid-eighteenth century not only displaced many Native American peoples, such as the Delaware and Shawnee, but it also threatened French commercial interests in the Ohio Valley and around the Great Lakes region. Trade relations between the settlers and the Native Americans were disrupted, with some tribes opting to break their associations with the French and form new ties with the British, while others attempted to strike the best deal between the competing Europeans.

By 1753, the French chose to protect their interests by constructing a series of forts from the Great Lakes to the Upper Ohio Valley. The British response consisted of a military expedition led by George Washington, supported by small numbers of Seneca, a campaign that spiralled out of control and led to a major British defeat at Fort Necessity on July 4, 1754, the French having bolstered their forces with Delaware, Ottawa, Algonquin, Wynadot and Abenaki allies. So began seven years of conflict as the two powers, plus their Native American allies, struggled for supremacy.

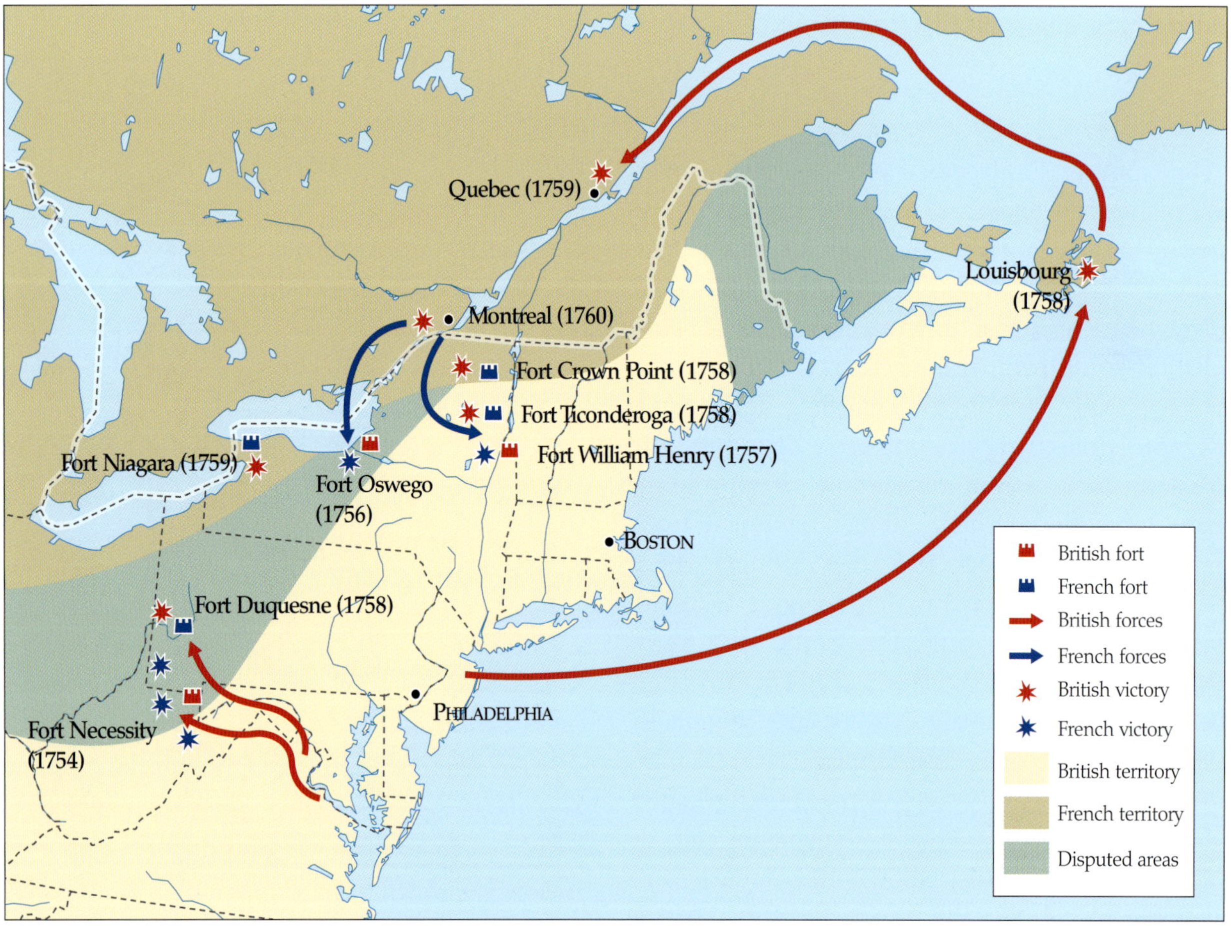

▲ **The French and Indian War saw major battles fought between the French and British across the American northwest. Being conducted across traditional Indian lands, the war was as significant for the Native Americans as the European powers.**

▲ **The massacre of British settlers, defeated by the French at Fort William Henry in August 1757, was a notorious episode. The French general, Marquis de Montcalm, tried to restrain his allies, but they killed up to 200 settlers, including children.**

From 1754–58, the French were largely the dominant force in the war, the British suffering major defeats at Fort Oswego (1756) and Fort William Henry (1757). Many Native Americans supported the French, inspired by their apparent ascendancy, and gained a brutal reputation—their massacre of civilians at Fort Oswego brought the lasting antipathy of many British settlers. British attempts to recruit their own Native American allies had mixed results: poor handling of Cherokee allies, for example, resulted in an Anglo–Cherokee War 1759–61. Yet in the late 1750s, the British started to send reinforcements and better commanders, and make firmer alliances with Iroquois tribes. From the autumn of 1758 until 1760, the French suffered a string of critical defeats, culminating in the losses of Quebec and Montreal. In 1763, the Treaty of Paris saw the French concede almost all their North American territories to the British. Native American tribes also suffered consequent loss of territory, and the Iroquois in particular lost their influence as intermediaries between the Europeans.

Pequot Warriors
This depiction of Pequot warriors in a canoe illustrates how tiny their "logistical footprint" was compared to European-style settler armies. This canoe, simply constructed from a dug-out tree trunk, could hold two or three men plus a basket and provisions but was light enough to carry on land when the warriors reached the shore.

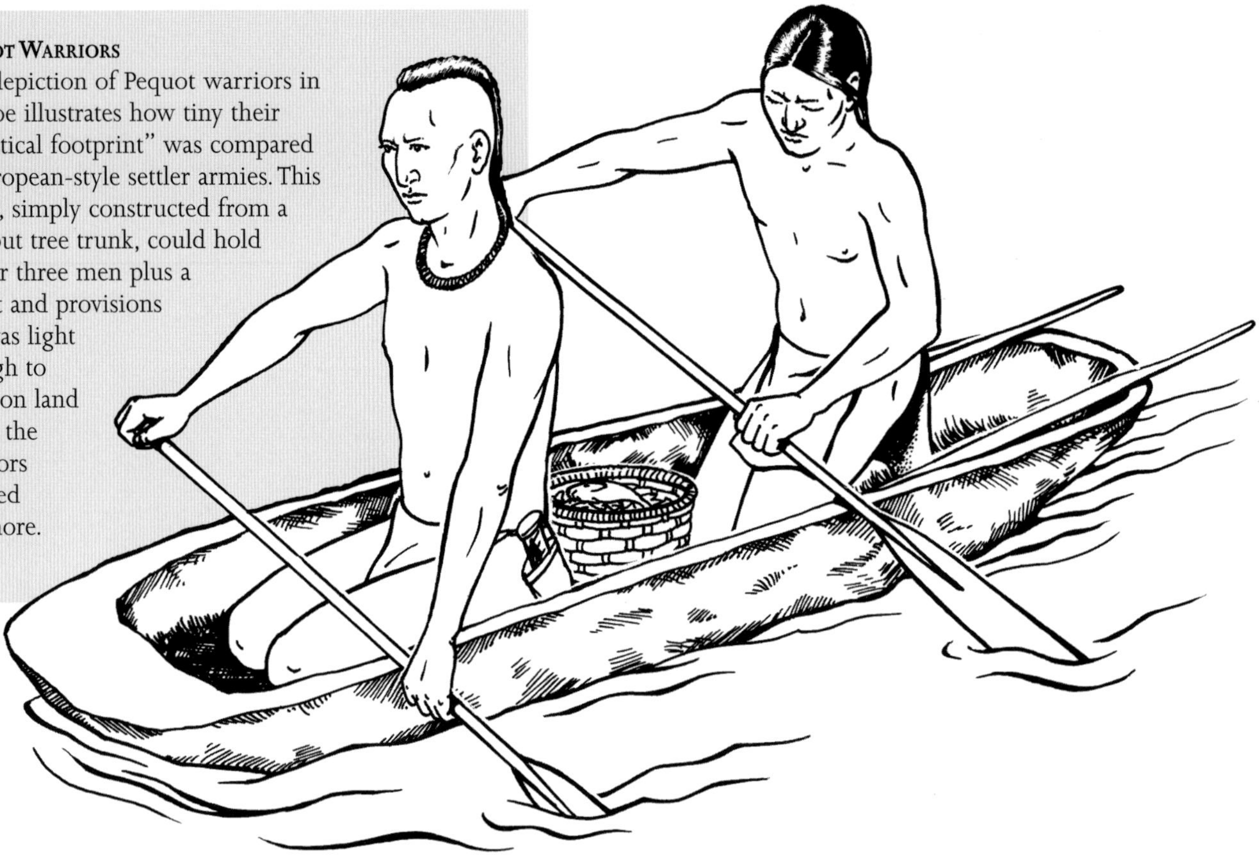

The Algonquian

The Algonquian-speaking nations also formed various confederacies, although with looser structures than that employed by the Iroquois. The less rigid organization was somewhat natural given the large numbers of Algonquian tribes, which included the Abenaki, Delaware, Mohegan, Narragansett, Pequot, Nanticoke, Algonquin and Shawnee. Like the Iroquois, the Algonquian confederacies had to adjust to the realities of colonial expansion during the seventeenth century, meeting them with a mix of compromise and military resistance. The fate of one of the alliances, the Powhatan Confederacy, is typical. Named after Chief Powhatan (this is his anglicized name—his real name was Wahunsunacock), the Powhatan Confederacy was formed at the beginning of the seventeenth century in Virginia and grew to a strength of 30 tribes. It has the dubious honor of being among the first Native American cultures to encounter the colonizing British, who put down permanent roots in Virginia in 1607 around Jamestown. In his 1781–82 work *Notes on the State of Virginia*, Thomas Jefferson noted in around 1607:

> "The territories of the Powhatan confederacy, south of the Patowmac, comprehended about 8000 square miles [20,720 square km], 30 tribes, and 2400 warriors. Capt. Smith tells us, that within 60 miles [96km] of James town were 5000 people, of whom 1500 were warriors. From this we find the proportion of their warriors to their whole inhabitants, was as 3 to 10. The Powhatan confederacy then would consist of about 8000 inhabitants, which was one for every square mile [2.5 square km]; being about the twentieth part of our present population in the same territory, and the hundredth of that of the British islands."

CHIEF POWHATAN

Known more properly as Wahunsunacock, Powhatan (c.1548–1618) was one of the great historical leaders of the Algonquian Native Americans. Powhatan was something of an opportunist—he initially negotiated and dealt with the British settlement around Jamestown, and was known to provide food to them on some occasions. He also made profitable alliances with the British to assist in his wars against other Native American tribes. Yet conversely, he saw that the settlers were intent on acquiring more land, which led to his formation of the Powhatan Confederacy. He launched several raids against the colonists but in 1614 his daughter, Pocahontas, married an English settler, John Rolfe, and for the next four years until his death in 1618 he was at peace with the British.

▼ An idealized image of Chief Powhatan communicating with the settlers. Here, he meets John Rolfe, who would marry his daughter, Pocahontas.

Cherokee in Traditional Outfit
A Cherokee male shows a mixture of functional and ceremonial items of dress, including a buckskin jacket with criss-crossing ornamental sash, a blanket or robe over one shoulder and soft moccasin shoes.

The evident strength of the Powhatan Confederacy enabled it to resist British attempts at subduing it, take on the Spaniards and also drive the rival Chesapeake tribe to destruction. Yet it was largely the great Powhatan himself who held the Confederacy together. By the time he died in 1618, he had established reasonably peaceful relations with the British settlers, but his efforts were utterly undone by his successor, his half-brother Opechancanough. Legitimately fearing British expansion, in March 1622 Opechancanough launched a massive strike against the British, killing nearly 350 colonists. Yet he had not counted on the European military response, and between 1622 and 1646 the British and the Powhatans found themselves locked in regular war. Using their superior firepower, the British forces inflicted a steadily mounting toll upon the tribes, although another major Native American attack on April 18, 1644 resulted in the death of a further 500 colonists. The British response was vigorous and violent, and by the spring of 1646, Opechancanough was captured

▲ **Captain John Smith taking Chief Opechancanough, war leader of the Pamunkey tribe, prisoner in 1646. Opechancanough was a major force in the Powhatan Wars and, after his capture, was murdered by a settler, angered by Opechancanough's "insurgency."**

and killed and large tracts of Algonquian land placed under British rule. The Powhatan Confederacy lasted only another four or five years before it finally broke part and its peoples dispersed.

The Southeast

In the Southeast culture area, there were more than 50 tribes at the time in contact with the colonial settlers. These tribes included the Alabama, Catawba, Cherokee, Chickasaw, Choctaw, Creek, Natchez and Seminole. The Cherokee are a particularly famous and interesting example of Native American warmaking. Spread across a wide region, from Virginia down to Georgia, the Cherokees were a generally independent collection of towns and villages until war threatened, when dedicated war chiefs would coordinate all the towns' efforts. The Cherokee first clashed with the settlers in 1654 when the Virginia Cherokee suffered a heavy defeat at the hands of settler infantry backed by Pamunkey Native Americans. Over the next 100 years, relations between the Cherokees and the colonists deteriorated into a state of regular war, culminating in the Cherokee War of 1759–61, which resulted in the tribe losing large parts of their territory in South and North Carolina to the British.

From the 1760s to the mid-1790s, the Cherokee were split into factions, some advocating peace with the settlers, while others prosecuted an insurgency against them. Yet in 1794, those resisting were largely defeated and Cherokee warriors even became auxiliary troops for American forces. Bad times were not over, however, and in 1835 the signing of the New Echota Treaty led to the expulsion of the Cherokee from their ancestral lands to the new Indian Territory in Oklahoma. The subsequent traumatic journey there became known as the Trail of Tears. The remainder of the nineteenth century saw the Cherokee torn apart by internal disputes, increased by wavering loyalties during the American Civil War, and the final story was largely one of dispossession. The story of the Cherokee was not unusual amongst the Native American tribes of the nineteenth century. Yet the overriding narrative of eventual defeat should not mask some of the impressive realities of the Native Americans in combat.

TRAIL OF TEARS Early 1800s

The Trail of Tears was an infamous act of inhumanity by the settlers towards the Native Americans. The Indian Removal Act of 1830 pushed Southeastern tribes from their centuries-old homelands out to new territories in the west. The displacement was often performed under military duress, and thousands died in transit or in harshly run settlements.

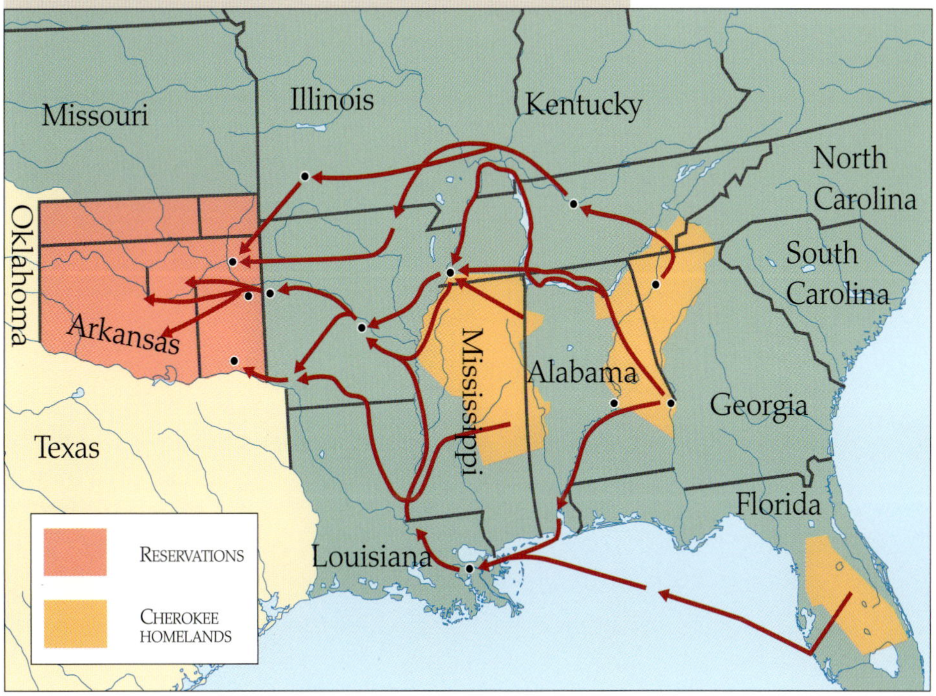

CHAPTER 2

Weapons

Before we study the actual warfighting tactics of the Eastern Native Americans, we must first appreciate the tools with which they fought. The most basic fighting weapon in terms of construction was the war club. There were several different styles. One featured a rounded ball-like head as the striking point, the head set forward of the haft. French clergyman Joseph Francois Lafitau (1681–1746) described it as "made of a tree root, or some other very hard wood, two or two and a half feet long [0.6–0.75m], squared on the sides, and widened or rounded to the width of a fist at its end" (quoted in Jones, 2004). An extant club from Massachusetts, dating back to the seventeenth century, was made from the ball root of a maple tree, and was elaborately decorated with white and purple *wampum* (*wampum* is bead decoration made from shells, typically those of whelks or clams). Other Eastern Native American club weapons more resembled wooden swords, with sharpened edges providing something of a cutting effect, or were fitted with antler, stone, bone or metal spikes to create a penetrating injury. Later clubs, known as gunstock clubs, were shaped in a similar fashion to a musket stock, with the addition of a metal blade to provide a cutting effect.

The Tomahawk

Related to the club was the tomahawk, today regarded as a defining weapon of the native Americans. The tomahawk is closely related to the Eastern Native Americans, the word coming from the Algonquian *otomahuk*, meaning "to strike down." At first, tomahawk heads were made from nothing more than shaped rock or a piece of soapstone, or a large section of bone, fastened to a haft measuring approximately 2 feet (0.6m) in length. The haft itself was made of a local wood such as hickory, maple or ash. Pipe tomahawks were made for ceremonial purposes by carving a pipe bowl into the poll of the axe, the smoke being drawn down the hollowed-out handle.

The effectiveness of the tomahawk was dramatically improved with the adoption of iron heads, which increased the weight, sharpness and durability of the blade. Such qualities were important,

▼ This warclub may have been intended for ceremonial purposes, on account of the decorated impact head. This club is of the older, ball-headed type, as opposed to the gunstock type often seen after settler contact.

◀ **Two examples of pipe tomahawks, one with a conventional axe blade (bottom), the other featuring a pick-type weapon. The introduction of steel by the settlers improved the tomahawk as a durable weapon.**

as the tomahawk was as much used for utility purposes, such as chopping wood and meat, as it was for combat. During a fight, however, the tomahawk was often thrown as well as being used hand-to-hand. A striking picture of the lethality of the tomahawk comes from an edition of the *New Monthly Magazine*, a collection of stories published in 1827. In an article entitled "A Canadian Campaign, by a British Officer" a British soldier recounts a major expedition against Native American tribes in the southeastern United States, and explains the following encounter:

"In this affair, I had an opportunity of particularly witnessing the cruel dexterity and despatch with which the Naive Americans use the tomahawk and scalping-knife. An American rifleman who had been dismounted within a few paces of the spot where I stood, was fired at by three warriors of the Delaware tribe. The unfortunate man received the several balls in his body, yet, though faint and tottering from loss of blood, he made every exertion to save himself. The foremost of his pursuers was a tall powerful man. When arrived within fifteen paces of his victim, uncovered in his flight, he threw his tomahawk, and with such force and precision, that it immediately opened the skull and extended him motionless on the earth. Laying down his rifle, he drew forth his knife, and after having removed the hatchet from the brain, proceeded to make a circular incision throughout the scalp. This done, he grasped the bloody instrument between his teeth, and placing his knees on the back of his victim, while at the same time he fastened his hands in the hair, the scalp was torn off without much apparent difficulty, and thrust still bleeding into his bosom. The warrior then arose, and after having wiped his knife on the clothes of the unhappy man, returned it to its sheath, grasping at the same time the arms he had abandoned, and hastening to rejoin his comrades. All this was the work of a minute."

This episode clearly illustrates the power of the tomahawk, as evidenced by its ability to bury itself into a man's skull. We also gain an insight into the terrible practice of scalping, about which more will be said in later chapters. Skill with the

THROWING A TOMAHAWK
Throwing a tomahawk required long hours of practice to perfect. For a distance of about 12 feet (3m), the thrower aimed to make the tomahawk describe one full revolution before striking the target, blade first. The more wrist flick applied, the faster the axe spun in the air, while a looser wrist slowed the spin.

tomahawk, however, took a long period of time to develop, as the hunter required a rapid and intuitive understanding of how many turns the tomahawk would make in flight so that it struck with the blade and not with another part of the weapon. Furthermore, if the tomahawk was his primary weapon, the Native American would find himself virtually defenceless once it had been thrown, hence in combat situations he was often more likely to use it as a hand-held weapon, taking advantage of its superiority when compared with the knife.

Daggers

By the eighteenth century, the Eastern Native Americans were increasingly using metal daggers as weapons of war. Prior to the arrival of the colonists, Native American blades were made largely of bone or rock, the latter "pressure-flaked" with the edge of an antler to form a rudimentary but dangerous blade. Some copper blades were manufactured, but with the arrival of the settlers the Native Americans began to purchase far more durable iron blades. A particularly popular style of knife was the "beaver tail" blade that, as its name suggests, had a broad double-edged blade tapering to an efficient point. The Native Americans developed gaudy sheaths to go with their blades, often encompassing hilt as well as blade, possibly suggesting that the knives were used more for utility and hunting than as a rapid-response weapon in combat. The Native Americans also made their own knives by sharpening up pieces of scrap metal and wrapping the "tang" (handle) with strips of hide to form a basic hilt.

Bows

Spears were common Native American weapons, at least up to around 1650, used for both fishing and hunting game. From the late seventeenth century onwards, however, spears were largely replaced for land hunting and warfare with firearms, although their practicality for fishing meant that their use did not die out altogether. Furthermore, Native American thrusting spears made poor weapons when compared to the metal-headed spears and pole arms brought into North America by the colonizing Europeans.

When faced by these, and the settlers' firearms, the bow and arrow made a far more equalizing weapons system. The exact type of bow used by Native Americans varied according to the tribe, available materials and the nature of the territory, but for the Eastern Native Americans, the most common type was the self-bow, meaning that the bow was made of a single piece of wood without the addition of pieces of sinew, horn, or bone.

Scalping

Scalping was one of the most notorious of Native American practices. The act could involve cutting away portions of skin, from a small disk of flesh around the crown of the skull, to the entire top portion of scalp, running from ear to ear. The scalps were retained as decorative, symbolic and ceremonial items, signifying the warrior's bravery.

▲ Native American warriors attacking an early seventeenth-century family of European settlers. Such depictions increased the hostility between white colonists and the Indian tribes living around the new settlements.

ARCHERS

The Eastern tribes used self-bows made from hickory, ash or locust wood. A typical length was about 67in (170cm), and arrows were tipped with either flint, bone or steel heads. The bow was accompanied by an arrow quiver, made from hide and often decorated with tassels.

Surrounded by plentiful supplies of high-quality woods, the Woodland Indians made a natural choice in their preference for self-bows, despite the fact that these traditionally have less power and range than composite or sinew-backed bows. Colin Taylor observes that there "is little question that the Woodland bow lacked the power of the traditional English longbow, with the Native American bow having of pull of up to 23kg (50lb), while the longbow pull could climb well beyond 32kg (70lb)" (Taylor, 2003).

Yet Taylor goes on to point out that the pull comparison is largely a paper exercise and that the difference in power lost much of its relevance in battle:

"Subsequent events, however, demonstrated that it [the Woodland bow] could have deadly effect at close range and in the hands of a skilled warrior. In 1636, when the Pequot killed several of Lion Gardiner's men at Fort Saybrook, Gardiner reported that 'the body of one man shot through, the arrow going in at the right side, the head sticking fast, half through a rib on the left side.' He sent both the arrow and the man's rib to officials in Massachusetts Bay Colony 'because they had said the arrows of the Indians were of no force.'"

– Taylor (2003)

Spears

These varied hugely in construction from simple sticks, sharpened with the point hardened over a fire, to carefully crafted missiles featuring flights and a separate flint spearhead bound onto the shaft by animal sinews. As this distinction suggests, Native American spears were broadly separated into two different categories—stabbing spears and throwing spears. The former were generally used to finish off injured game, while the latter served as a ranged weapon against dangerous animals, or enemies. The range and penetration of a throwing spear could be increased by the use of the atlatl, a spear-throwing device. This was essentially a hooked stick about 18 inches (45cm) long into which the heel of the spear was slotted. By throwing the spear forwards using the atlatl, the user could increase the acceleration applied to it, and hence improve its distance and power. However, the space required to use the atlatl effectively meant that it was less popular among the Eastern territories, with its dense woodlands, than it was further out west and in the subarctic north, where open spaces and large prey such as buffalo meant the spear thrower could be used to its full potential.

▲ A settler engraving shows Native American youths shooting arrows and throwing balls at targets and engaging in running races. Athleticism and warrior skills were taught from infancy.

As discussed, the Woodland bow had plenty of power within its effective range. Its penetration was further enhanced by the quality of its arrows. The arrow shafts themselves were made from canes or bones, smoothed out with a knife or scraper to remove any imperfections. Arrowheads were crafted from a variety of materials, such as shards of stone, flint or bone, or pieces of shell, wood, horn or antler. The arrowhead would be set in a split at the end of the shaft, and lashed into place with sinew, rawhide or plant material. However, sometimes the head would be set loose in the shaft so that it would detach in a prey or enemy

Spear Points
A collection of flint arrowheads from the Eastern Woodlands, dating back to prehistoric times. Some arrowheads were loosely attached to the arrow shaft, causing them to detach inside prey and produce more serious injuries over time.

to increase the complications, hence the severity, of the wound.

Practical combat range in the confined woods and forests of the Eastern territories did not require a bow that could shoot out to hundreds of metres. Woodland warriors attempted to close the distance between themselves and their enemy as much as possible before taking the shot—this mirrored how they practised hunting. In addition, after a lifetime of practice they could deliver the arrows to the target with astonishing accuracy. Daniel Harman, a partner in the North West Company in 1808, explained how the Cree Native Americans, whose territories butted up against the eastern regions, began honing their bow skills from infancy:

"Their youth, from the age of four or five to that of eighteen or twenty years, pass nearly half of their time in shooting arrows at a mark ... From so early and constant a practice, they become, at length, the best marksmen, perhaps, in the world. Many of them, at a distance of eight or ten rods [a rod is equivalent to 16ft 6in/5m], will throw an arrow with such precision, as twice out of three times, to hit a mark the size of a dollar."

– Daniel Harman (1808)

Atlatl Throwing Technique
The atlatl was a simple device for increasing the acceleration behind a spear throw. Note how the warrior first uses the momentum of a run, then a deep lunge, to apply his full body weight to the throw. The whipping action of the atlatl greatly amplifies this force.

Firearms

In addition to accuracy, it could be argued that for a significant period of time, arguably from 1500 until the nineteenth century, bows actually delivered superior firepower when compared to the muzzle-loading firearms of the time. A flintlock musket, even in well-trained hands, was only capable of around two or three aimed shots every minute, less once the gun had become fouled during battle. The bow, however, could shoot an arrow every 10 seconds and had no problems with fouling, damp powder or an imperfect flint. The only drawback of the bow when compared to the musket was that the former took years of practice to perfect, whereas a few weeks' instruction with a firearm would bring enough practical, if not expert, proficiency.

Of course, in time, guns would change everything for the Eastern Native Americans as for the other Native Americans of the United States. The Eastern Native Americans were the first to encounter firearms, and were undoubtedly impressed by their flash and thunder, if not by their performance. On July 29, 1609, the French explorer Samuel de Champlain, along with a party of a few Europeans and about 60 allied Native American warriors, were confronted by a war party of about 200 Iroquois or Mohawks. De Champlain loaded four balls into his matchlock arquebus and fired at his opponents—the single shot killed two enemy chiefs and wounded another man. Such was the surprise that the war party retreated and dispersed.

Once the shock of the new had worn off, however, the Eastern Native Americans began purchasing guns from the settlers. They used these firearms to settle

tribal scores, hence the Cree and the Chippewa Native Americans were able to force the Sioux out from the western regions of the Eastern Woodlands around 1700, and push them towards the plains that would become their homeland. The Mohawk performed similar feats against the Delaware Confederation.

At first, the firearms bought by the Native Americans were matchlock arquebus types, the powder in the pan detonated by a glowing match. The matchlock mechanism was not suited to hunting—the light and the smell generated by the match gave the user's presence away to sensitive game animals—and its unreliability in damp woodland conditions meant that the bow was still king.

The balance changed slightly in the second half of the seventeenth century, when more reliable flintlock weapons became available to the Native Americans through British, Dutch and French traders. Ironically, the Native Americans actually proved more skilful in the use of firearms than their suppliers; a lifetime of training in accurate bow shooting translated into generally excellent musket marksmanship. Later on, by the early nineteenth century, the Native Americans sought to acquire rifled instead of smoothbore firearms, appreciating the additional range and accuracy of such weapons.

▲ An Indian Wars reenactor shows a typical flintlock firearm. The Eastern Indians found flintlock firearms more practical than the Plains Indians, as they mostly fought on foot rather than horseback.

CHAPTER 3

Armor

Although the Native Americans are popularly seen either bare-chested or wearing loose, soft garments, they also had their own armor. Shields, for example, were common pieces of war-fighting kit amongst the Eastern tribes. In the northeast, the shields tended to be fairly plain and unadorned, but they came in a wide spectrum of types.

Some were constructed from a wooden section of willow or similar wood and wrapped with animal skins, while others might consist of nothing more than multiple layers of leather formed into a square shield with a handgrip at the back. The historian David E. Jones explains some of the other varieties found in the northeast:

"The Wampanoag warriors of Cape Cod used shields made of bark slabs (Steel [1994]). The Huron warrior carried one of two types—one a small rawhide shield and the other of bark and almost large enough to cover a man's body. The Miamis' shields were made of buffalo rawhide. Long rawhide shields are reported for the Potawatomi, Illinois and Ottawa (Pritzker [1998], 2). The Lenape in Pennsylvania and Delaware preferred large wooden or moose rawhide shields (ibid)."

– *Jones* (2004)

A similar wide variety of war shields was seen in the southeastern territories, including wicker shields. Although wicker is itself a fairly insubstantial material, contemporary accounts indicate that in the shields it was so tightly woven that arrows would not penetrate. (Jones notes that the Spanish discovered that even crossbow bolts were unable to punch through the wicker shields.)

In combat, the warrior might grip the shield with his left hand (or vice versa), positioning it to protect his torso while leaving his right hand free to wield a tomahawk or knife. Archers might also hang the shield from one of their shoulders while taking a shot, in so doing protecting an exposed side of the body.

In addition to shields, the Eastern Native Americans also had numerous varieties of body

Iroquois with Flintlock Musket
An Iroquois warrior stands with a crudely contoured "trade gun" musket. The Northeastern Indians tended to use firearms modelled more on French types, as the Indians were familiar with these from the early days of European settlement. Note that this warrior wears a small section of slat armor over the groin area.

BREASTPLATE
An elaborate armored breastplate, featuring two sections composed of wooden rods and slats bound tightly together with rawhide cord. Such armor provided decent protection for centuries before the arrival of the settlers. Once the settlers came, however, armor was made increasingly redundant by the penetrative power of firearms.

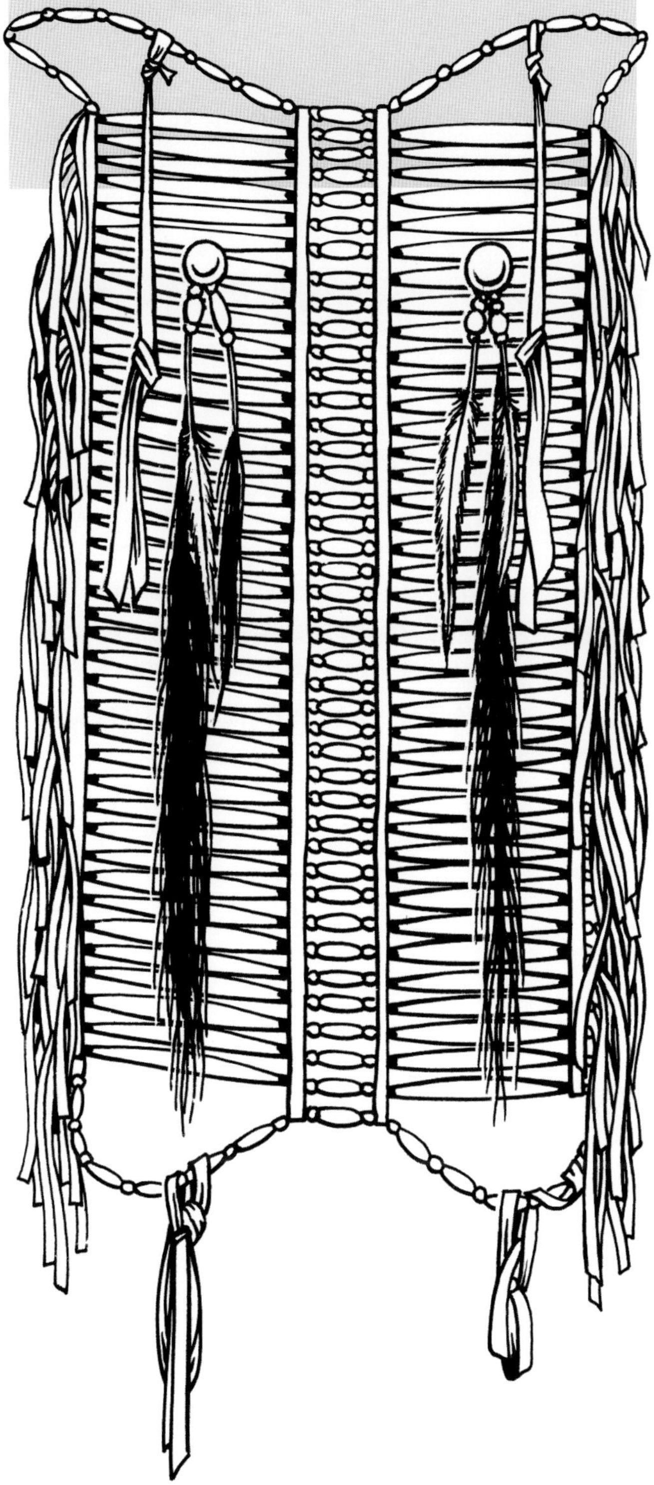

armor, although the pattern of distribution varies according the region. In the northeast, the armor was typically made of slats or rods of wood, bone, wicker or rawhide, the whole structure sewn together with rawhide and worn as a form of breastplate via a strap around the neck. Alternatively, the armor might be made from a single piece of wood and wrapped in thick material as padding. Separate pieces could be added to the armor to protect the back and the upper portions of the legs. Although little seen in visual records, some literary sources also refer to the Iroquois wearing helmets, produced from hoops of branches or wicker and bound together with twine.

Travelling further south, references to body armor become fewer, although not completely absent. Some illustrations show a gorget worn around the neck, basically a disk of wood, shell, slate or even metal about 10 inches (25cm) across and hung over the upper chest, although the primary purpose of this device may well have been ceremonial rather than protective.

Prior to the introduction of firearms, the Native American armor and shields would have been capable of stopping most arrows and hand-thrown spears. The introduction of guns, however, changed matters irrevocably. Apart from against the heaviest shields, musket balls fired from later firearms (from the eighteenth century onwards) would typically penetrate a wicker breastplate or buffalo hide shield. In consequence, armor was largely irrelevant by the nineteenth century, and was relegated to ceremonial usage.

CHAPTER 4

Fortifications

Fortifications are a little-appreciated aspect of Native American warfare. The Native Americans were surrounded by a dangerous world, every village and community being threatened by raids or more substantial attacks. In response, the Eastern Native Americans (and others, as we shall see) sometimes fortified their permanent villages or camps, producing edifices of genuine defensive sophistication.

By 1500, the single-wall palisade defence, sometimes with a wet or dry ditch surrounding it, had evolved into fortifications with two, three or four concentric palisades, the palisades formed from thick poles. The palisades could rise 30 feet (9m) high, and the ground between them was laid with tree trunks to provide a form of walkway, or were criss-crossed with flexible boughs, bound together at the top with rawhide to form another obstacle to movement, should anyone manage to penetrate the outer defences. Above the palisades rose watchtowers and defensive galleries, used as fighting platforms from which rocks, arrows, missiles and gunfire could be directed at any attacking forces.

Some of the best descriptions of Native American fortifications come from French observers. One of them, Joseph Lafitau, writing in the eighteenth century, provides an excellent and detailed description of an Iroquois outpost:

"The villages most vulnerable to hostile forces are fortified by a palisade 15–20ft [4.5–6m] high, composed of three rows of posts, those in the middle set straight and perpendicular, the others crossing each other at an angle like saw-bucks, reinforced by heavy, dense bark to the height of 10 or 12ft [3–3.5m]. Inside this palisade, the Indians have ordered a kind of gallery or circular walk created by trees laid horizontally, all joining the palisade and set on large forked posts of wood stuck into the ground. At regular intervals, there are redoubts or watch towers, which in times of war are filled up with stones to defend against scaling attacks and for pouring water to put out fire. They [the defenders] climb up there using steps cut into the trunks of trees which act as ladders.

▲ **An Eastern Canadian Native American dressed in traditional dress, dancing and taking part in a pow-wow (a council or meeting of Indians). As well as carrying many ceremonial items, he wears a long breastplate of slat armor, which was traditionally made of wood, reed or pieces of bone.**

The palisade also has openings cut into it to serve as battlements. The nature of the terrain determines the shape of their enclosures. They are sometimes shaped as polygons, but the largest number are round or spherical in shape ... The palisade has only one exit, via a narrow door set at a slant, closing with a cross bar, through which people have to pass sideways."

– *Lafitau* (1724)

The structure of this fortification, as described by Lafitau, must have presented a genuine challenge to any attacker, especially with significant fire coming from the battlements. In fact, often the attacking force would avoid attacking the fortification at all, instead taunting the occupants until some of them ventured outside and were killed or injured, at which point the attackers would consider their job done.

Yet although the fortifications were undoubtedly a fearsome proposition for attack by Native Americans in the pre-firearms arm, there were some contemporary European observers who gave them little value in the Early Modern age. Writing in 1653, the Dutch New Netherland landowner, Adriaen Cornelissen van der Donck, acknowledged the intelligent structural set-up of the local Northeast Native American fortifications, but draws a sceptical conclusion:

"In the villages and castles they always do solid and good work. As sites for their castles they tend to prefer, if possible, a high or steep hill near water or a riverside, which is difficult to climb up and often accessible on one side only. They always take care also that it is flat and even on top. This they enclose with a very heavy wooden stockade constructed in a peculiar interlocking diamond pattern. First they lay a heavy tree along the ground on both sides, which forms a cross at the upper end where they are notched to fit tighter together. Next another tree is laid in there to make a very solid work. The palisades stand two deep, sufficiently strong to protect them from a surprise attack or sudden raid by their enemies, but they do not as yet have any knowledge of properly equipping such a work with curtains, bastions, and flanking walls. They also build some small forts here and there on the level and low land near their plantations to shelter their wives and children from an assault, in case they have enemies so nearby that they could be fallen upon by small parties. They think highly of their forts and castles built in that fashion, but these actually are of little consequence, and cause them more harm than good in war with the Christians."

– *Snow et al.* (1996)

Van der Donck highlights the fact that it was not the fortification alone that presented the challenge for the war party; the location of the fortified village would ideally add to its security. Yet his statement at

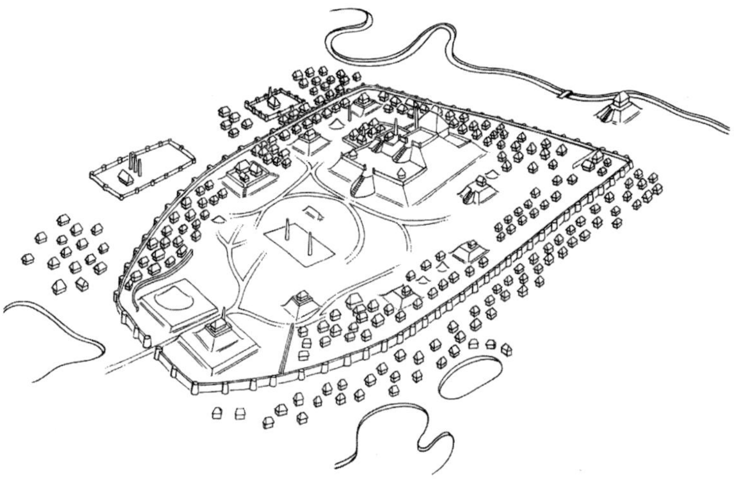

COHOKIA FORT
The Cohokia Fort, located near Collinsville, Illinois, is a fine example of early Native American fort building. It featured an extensive outer palisade that wrapped around many of the settlement's habitations. Acting almost like a medieval European bailey was a massive terraced "mound" capped by a ceremonial temple building. Although the Cohokia Fort lapsed into disuse just before 1500, it illustrates that defensive sophistication was part of Indian culture even before the settlers arrived.

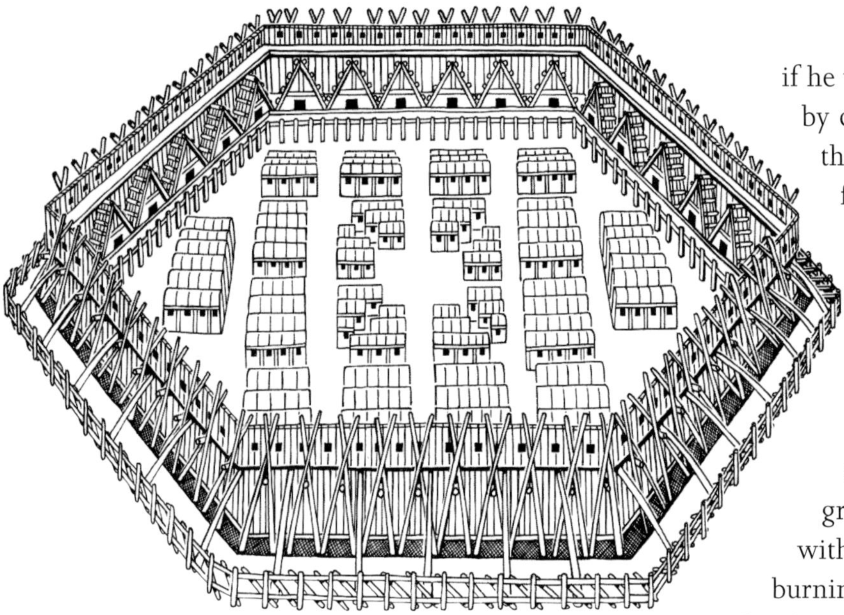

if he were to avoid his forces being devastated by crossfire or fire to his rear. Furthermore, the Chickasaw shot flaming arrows into flammable outlying structures, the resulting smoke making the French efforts even more complicated, resulting in an eventually ineffective attack. Bienville, in an official report back to France, also pointed out that Native Americans fought from shoulder-high holes dug into the ground, and would cover defensive cabins with "a wall of earth and wood proof against burning arrows and grenades so that nothing but bombs can harm them" (see Jones [2004]). Such was the nature of Native American

Iroquois Fortification
This diagrammatic representation of an Iroquois fortification illustrates the sophistication of Native American defensive design. The outer defences consist of a low palisade, then a stretch of ground, broken up by poles, before the main defensive walls. The stretch of open ground served as a killing area for the defenders, who fired bows and firearms as the attackers struggled for entry.

the end that, in effect, the fortifications were strategically pointless should not be taken at face value, and appears to be European condescension. Certainly, the introduction of heavy artillery into American warfare would seem to pose a significant threat to a lashed wooden structure. The work of historian David Jones, however, throws Van der Donck's perspective into question. He describes how the French around New Orleans, led by Governor Bienville, allied themselves with the Choctaw Native Americans in an effort to defeat the belligerent Chickasaw tribe.

The first problem that confronted Bienville was that the fortified village of Ackia, his main target, was protected by two other hill forts. This mutually supportive defensive arrangement meant that Bienville had to tackle all three strongpoints at once

▲ **A seventeenth-century engraving shows Native American raiders, armed with bows and firearms, setting fire to the town of Deerfield in Franklin County, Massachusetts.**

Creek Village
This Creek Indian village is protected mainly by an outer forest—Indian scouts and guard dogs would typically alert the occupants to any intruders (particularly heavy-footed settlers) before they even arrived. The Indians occupy wood-framed houses, insulated with foliage, and animal fodder is stored behind in a fenced area. The warrior in the center carries a matchlock musket.

fortifications that the colonists required major artillery resources if they were to attack them in a direct assault. Jones points to an official Ministry of the Colonies letter dated January 1, 1739, which reveals the ordnance required by an attacking army to effectively take on a fortified Chickasaw village:

"As for the artillery, since the Chickasaw villages that are to be attacked are fortified, it was thought advisable to send four eight-pounder cannon; eight four-pounders, six of which carry ammunition for three shots; two nine-pounder mortars of brass; two of iron of six-pound caliber; twelve other small mortars of wrought-iron which were forged for this purpose; and powder, bullets, bombs and the tools necessary to make use of them."

This list shows that the artillery deemed necessary to take on the Native American village is substantial, indicating that cracking a Native American fort was not casual matter for European colonists, even equipped as they were with the modern engines of war.

Yet despite the evidence that extensive firepower was necessary, and to be fair to Van der Donck's views given earlier, in the grand totality of the campaigns of the Eastern Native Americans to preserve their native territories, the fortifications did not ultimately succeed. Why this is so will be address in the next section.

CHAPTER 5

Tactics

"Indisciplined" Warfare

As already noted in the Introduction, Native American warmaking was very different to that of the European settlers. Typically, colonial interpretations of Native American warfare and tactics emphasized native "indiscipline," as compared to the ordered ranks and hierarchical structure of European-style armies. Yet history has consistently shown us that the Native American warriors actually possessed discipline in plentiful supply, but just of a different manner. Armstrong Starkey, writer of the study *European and Native American Warfare* 1675–1815, has commented on this different type of martial discipline:

"In contrast to European armies, Indian discipline was founded on individual honor rather than corporal punishment; leaders were chosen according to merit based on courage and experience instead of privilege or purchase. Commanders were concerned to save their men's lives and believed that victory did not justify unnecessary sacrifice. There was no disgrace in retreating to await a more favorable occasion for battle. Indian leaders taught their men to move in scattered order and take advantage of the ground, to surround the enemy or to avoid being surrounded. They practised running and marksmanship and they became accustomed to endure hunger and hardship with patience and fortitude."

– *Starkey* (1998)

Starkey describes a type of discipline and intelligence that would be far more appreciable to modern special forces, rather than the tradition-bound ranks of Revolutionary War European armies.

Looking at the Eastern Native Americans specifically, this instinctive discipline expressed itself in warfare

WOODLAND ARCHER
This simply dressed Eastern Indian takes up an ambush position. Note how he grips an arrow in each hand to facilitate quick reloading—a trained warrior would be able to fire an aimed shot every seven or eight seconds. As a backup weapon, he wears a dagger on his waist, the blade probably purchased from the settlers.

in several ways. First, as Starkey notes, the Native Americans made excellent use of terrain. From their experience of hunting in the woodlands, the Eastern warriors prioritized stealthy deployment of their forces into good ambush positions or places from which a sudden attack could be launched. In essence, they followed modern procedures of cover and concealment by using hills, depressions, rivers, dense foliage and other natural features to stay out of sight until the moment to attack came. Moreover, the war party would often move through this terrain in loose order (another reason why the Europeans interpreted them as indisciplined), each man taking his own route while being instinctively aware of the others around him. As with hunting, the war party members would try to maneuver themselves so that the enemy (the prey) were trapped and had no easy route of escape. Often one group would act as a primary attacking force, while another set up an ambush position along the enemy's line of retreat to hit them as they fell back.

The experience for the victims of a Native American ambush could be disconcerting to say the least. Daniel Gookin (1612–87), a settler who lived in Virginia and Massachusetts and wrote extensively on the Native Americans and their practices, explained how actually fighting against the Native Americans quickly cured the settlers of any misconceptions:

AMBUSH
A group of Native American raiders move into ambush position overlooking a colonial settlement and its valuable livestock. They take advantage of the settlement's outer perimeter fence to conceal their movements. The warriors might wait in this position for hours, withholding their attack until the first light of dawn or an opportunity for surprise.

▲ **Woodland Indians were masters of stealth and concealment, skills learned from years of hunting. Here a re-enactor illustrates how a deer skin could be used to break up the warrior's silhouette.**

"But it was found another manner of thing than expected; for our man could see no enemy to shoot at, but yet felt their bullets out of the thick bushes where they lay in ambushments. The enemy also used this strategem, to apparel themselves from the waist upwards with green boughs, that our Englishman could not readily discern them from the natural bushes; this manner of fighting our men had little experience of, and hence they were under great disadvantage."

Gookin's quotation highlights the fact that the Woodland Indians were also masters of camouflage, using green leafy bows or animal skins to blend in with their terrain, and break up their silhouettes to enemy musketeers. A nineteenth-century account of a Virginia rifleman on guard duty on the Plains of

Battles in the East
1777–1858

The map below illustrates some of the major engagements fought between the Native Americans and the settlers from 1777 to 1858. Initially, the Indians in the east had the tactical advantage, but weight of settler numbers and attrition gradually took their toll. By the late 1850s, all of the Eastern territories were subdued by the settlers, the Native American tribes either destroyed, displaced further west or relocated onto reservations. The year 1858 saw the final subjugation of the Seminole, after a series of three wars.

Chippewa during the French and Indian War speaks of the audacity with which the Eastern Native American could apply his camouflage skills:

"At length, a low rustling among the bushes on the right caught his ear. He gazed long towards the spot whence the sound seemed to proceed, but saw nothing, save the impenetrable gloom of the thick forest which surrounded the encampment. Then, as he marched onward, he heard o'er the gentle breeze of night, the joyful cry of 'all's well', after which, he seated himself upon a stump, and dropped in a deep fit of musing. While he thus sat, a Savage entered the open space behind him, and, after buckling his tunic, with its numerous folds, tight around his body, drew over his head the skin of a wild boar, with the natural appendages of these animals; and, thus accoutred, walked slowly past the soldier, who, seeing the object approach, quickly stood upon his guard. But a well-known grunt eased his fears, and he suffered it to pass, it being too dark for any one to discover the cheat. The beast quietly sought the thicket to the left; it was nearly out of sight, when through a sudden break in the clouds, the moon shone bright upon it. The soldier then perceived the ornamental moccasin of a Savage, and quick as thought prepared to fire. But, fearing lest he might have been mistaken, and thus falsely alarm the camp—and also supposing, if it were so, other Savages would be near at hand, he refrained, and, having a perfect knowledge of Indian subtility, quickly took off his coat and cap, and, after hanging them on the stump where he had reclined, took hold of his rifle, and

◀ King Philip, also known as Metacom, leader of the Wampanoag Indians, led his tribe during the bitter King Philip's War of 1675–76. The bold Indian attempt to drive out the settlers from Massachusetts initially succeeded, but the tide turned in 1675 and it is estimated that by the time defeat came, 15 percent of the Wampanoag had been killed.

softly groped his way towards the thicket. He had barely reached it, when the whizzing of an arrow passed his head, and told him of the danger he had so narrowly escaped."

– Turner (1836)

The techniques employed by the Indian here would not disgrace a modern special forces sniper, and only the American soldier's quick-thinking appears to have saved his life. Furthermore, the Indians were more prepared to use daylight and seasonal conditions to aid their operations. For example, when Narragansett Indians aided the English in an attack on a local Pequot camp, they moved in at night, when the Pequot would be unprepared and mostly confined in their homes.

The Battle of Bloody Brook

A good example of how effective the Woodland Indians could be in ambush comes from King Philip's War (1675–76), one of the bloody seventeenth-century conflicts that blighted relations between the Native Americans and the New England colonists. The conflict also provides a useful insight into how the wars between Indians and settlers often progressed. Its causes were familiar enough—settler expansionism, Christian proselytizing, then the collapse of local trade relations brought Chief Philip of the Wampanoag tribe into conflict with the British settlers in Massachusetts. A particular grievance of the Wampanoag was the foundation of the town of Swansea, located just 4 miles (6.4km) away from Philip's home settlement, in the mid-1660s. On June 20, 1675, Wampanoag warriors attacked Swansea, and so began a round of tit-for-tat violence that would roll on for more than a year.

A notable action during the war was the battle of Bloody Brook, fought on September 18, 1675. It provides a textbook example of the effectiveness of Indian assault tactics. The burgeoning war had resulted in many colonists having to evacuate their towns, which were classed as at risk of falling to the Indians. Unfortunately, the very act of evacuation presented the Wampanoag with superb opportunities for ambush against the slow-moving columns of soldiers and civilians. One such column was led by Captain Thomas Lathrop, who was escorting a load of cut wheat bound for the town of Hadley, where a British garrison was helping to provide protection for villages and evacuees. The route to their journey took them through an area of swampland 10km (6 miles) south of the town, bisected by a brook—perfect ambush terrain in which the Indians concealed themselves ready for action. Swampland of any description was always threatening to the settlers, as it dramatically slowed movement while the Indians themselves moved around the landscape easily in their soft moccasins, which served to deaden the noise of footfalls. An early British settler in Massachusetts, Samuel Gorton, had actually described swampland as "more pernicious to valiant souldiers then are bullwarkes, towers, castles, and walled cities." It was a dangerous place through which to move, but there was complacency among the British ranks. The British column was a substantial one, and Lathrop had 80 soldiers under his command, all armed with muskets. Yet as the column slowed to cross the brook, a force of Wampanoag warriors suddenly burst from their hiding places around the swamp and opened a withering fire upon the British soldiers, using well-

▼ Lithograph of Arthur St. Clair's Defeat (1791), in the opening stages of the battle with North American Indians near Fort Wayne, Ohio. The battle was a major Indian victory, leaving some 600 Americans dead.

aimed musket fire and archery. During the attack, the Indians illustrated the classic principles of Native American firepower—spot a target, shoot it, then get back into cover while selecting another target. In this instance, such was the confidence of the fire that some 64 colonists were killed.

The noise of the exchange brought nearby British reinforcements, a unit of infantrymen led by Major Robert Treat and Captain Samuel Moseley, supported by a band of Mohegan Native Americans. Yet at this point the other element of Native American warfare came into play—the tactical retreat. Rather than engage the superior force, and with the element of surprise lost, they simply vanished back into the wilderness. The British soldiers moved back to Deerfield, where during the night they could hear the Indians taunting them from nearby woodland. In the end, Deerfield was simply abandoned and the town was burnt to the ground.

The Battle of the Wabash

Perhaps the most illustrative example of Native Americans dominating regular forces came at the Battle of the Wabash (also known as St. Clair's Defeat) on November 4, 1791. The context to the battle was the 1783 Treaty of Paris, which placed the territory east and south of the Great Lakes under US sovereignty. Naturally, the local Native Americans were not party to the treaty, and so began a campaign of regular violence against the Americans, with 1500 white settlers killed during the second half of the 1780s. Finally, the government of President Washington had had enough, and assembled a force of 1453 regular soldiers to go out and crush the Indian insurrection, the formation marching on October 7, 1790 commanded by Brigadier General Josiah Harmar. Battle was first joined near present-day Fort Wayne, Indiana, when some 400 American soldiers crossed swords with 1100 Indians, Harmar refusing to commit his full resources. The result was 223 American casualties, and the first defeat of the campaign. Indian casualties were similar, but they had taken the tactical initiative and put a severe dent in American martial confidence.

The next year, therefore, Washington ordered a renewed offensive, this time under the command of Arthur St. Clair, a capable Seven Years' War veteran and governor of the Northwest territories. St. Clair had a total of 2000 men, but they were of indifferent quality. Desertion cost his command 1800 men between September and November 1791. Many of the soldiers were part-time militia with scant experience of weapons handling and poor understanding of tactics and woodland survival. At dawn break on November 4, 1791, the motley force was encamped near what is today Fort Recovery, Ohio, near the Wabash River, unaware that a confederacy of some 1000 Native American warriors—Cherokee, Chippewas, Shawnees, Delawares, Mingos and others, led by the chiefs Little Turtle and Blue Jacket—was watching them and waiting to attack.

Devastating Attack

When the attack came, it was devastating. The Native American forces surged down to the perimeter of the American lines, using cover and concealment all the way. They set up a withering and accurate musket fire, thinning the ranks of the Americans as the regular soldiers and militia grabbed for their own stacked muskets. The American troops finally managed to establish some manner of traditional defensive line, and sent volleys of fire hissing through the undergrowth. They even managed to bring some cannon fire into play, although the canister shot flew too high, and simply went over the heads of the attacking Indians. Whatever firepower the Americans could generate had little effect—a musket ball could not get through the thick trees and earthen banks that the Indians were using for fire positions. Moreover, the attackers had deployed in a loose U-shaped formation around the American camp, and did not present the uniform ranks that were the best targets for volley fire.

Sensing their defeat, the American soldiers mounted a bayonet charge, but in response the Indians simply fell back and then circled around to cut off the charging soldiers from the camp. Eventually St. Clair—one of the few officers left alive, although he had

Shawnee Warrior
This Shawnee Indian warrior is dressed in a style typical of the eighteenth and nineteenth centuries. A cotton shirt provides the base garment, with an overwrapped blanket for warmth. The hair style—shaven except for a tuft of hair left on the crown—often incorporated braided locks and feather decoration. He carries a self-bow and three metal-tipped arrows.

Mohawk Warrior
This Mohawk warrior, bearing traditional facial tattoos, wears a metal gorget around his neck and has a dagger in a scabbard attached to his cross-straps. The pouch on the hip would have contained powder and balls for the flintlock musket, plus other supplies.

nearly been killed on several occasions—finally ordered a retreat, and those that could fled into the surrounding woodlands. The action had been a spectacular victory for the Indians—600 Americans dead as opposed to 21 Indians—and a dose of reality for the US military.

The Second Seminole War

Throughout the seventeenth, eighteenth and nineteenth centuries, the Indians consistently played to their strengths against the Americans weaknesses. Although the were unable to "win the war," they nevertheless secured enough victories in battle to trouble the settlers seriously. This was evident in the series of three Seminole Wars fought in Florida between 1816 and 1858, focused on the US government's attempts to control, subdue or expel the Seminole Indians from their traditional lands. The Second Seminole War of 1835–42 is particularly interesting from a tactical perspective, not least because of the abilities of one of the Seminole leaders, Osceola. Osceola's leadership skills comprehensively dismiss the idea that Indian warfare was

Osceola (c.1803–38)
Born into the Seminole in circa 1803, Osceola gained early experience of combat fighting in the First Seminole War (1816–18), and rose to become a tribal leader by the early 1830s. During this time, Osceola resisted the US government's efforts to shift his people to Indian Territory (Oklahoma) and killed some prominent Seminole leaders who advocated the relocation. Osceola led his tribe in a guerilla war against the Americans for two years, inflicting serious casualties on the settlers through intelligent guerrilla warfare. In October 1837, however, he was duped into attending apparent peace discussions with the US commander General Thomas Jesup and was arrested upon his arrival. He was imprisoned near Charleston and died there on January 30, 1838.

Horseshoe Bend 1814

The battle of Horseshoe Bend in 1814 was a major Native American defeat in the Creek War (1813–14). Assisted by a large group of Cherokee Indians, future US president Andrew Jackson led a force of US troops against a Red Sticks Creek encampment in the Horseshoe Bend of the Tallapooa River. While the US soldiers formed the "hammer" from the north, the allied Indians created the "anvil" to the south, resulting in 750 Red Sticks killed out of a total force of 900 warriors.

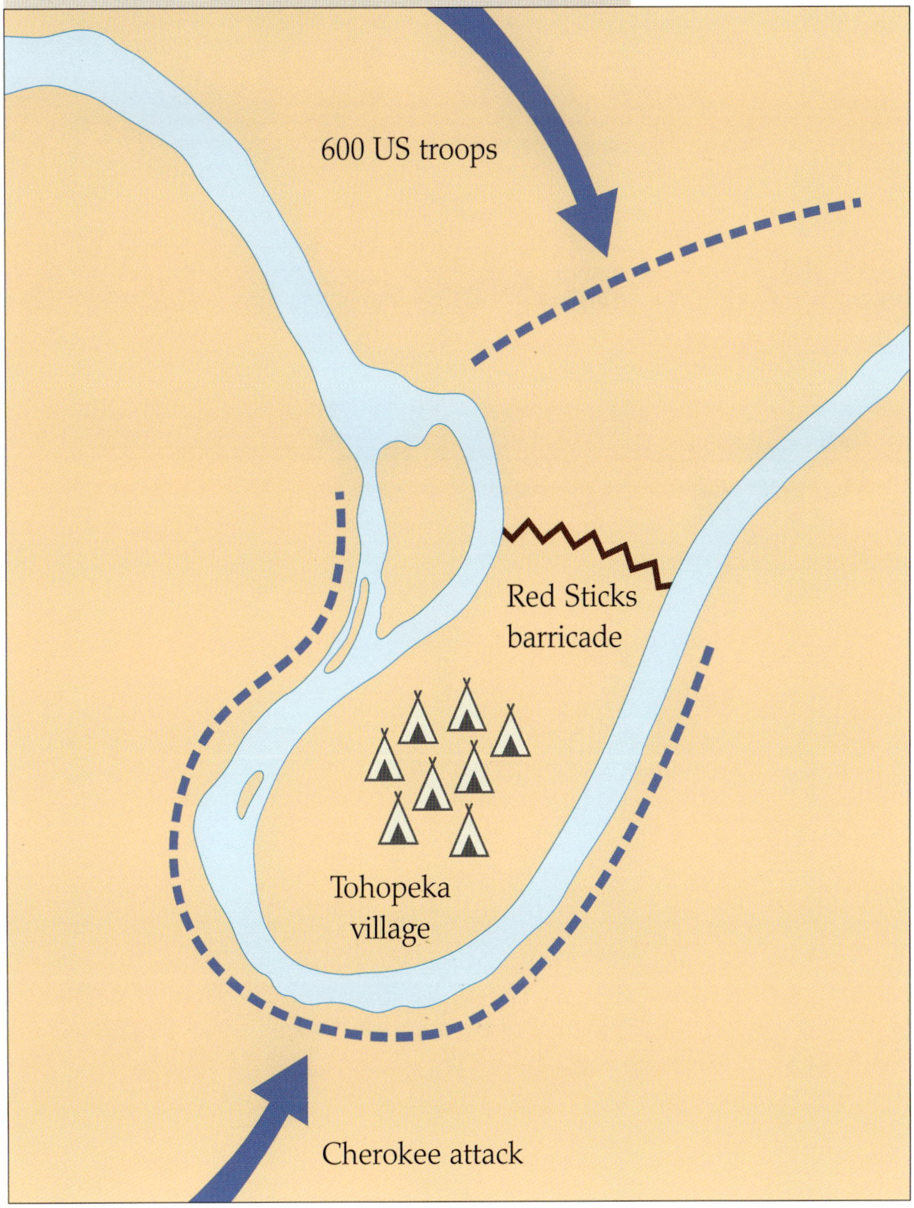

rudimentary. Indeed, he seems to combine the Indian skills of guerrilla warfare with a more conventional understanding of how to inflict maximum damage on the enemy's ability to wage war.

For example, Osceola recognized that the various Seminole tribes would be much more effective if they coordinated their activities, so established a system of assistant commanders and of rapid inter-tribal communications, which allowed him to channel his forces quickly against emerging weak points. Furthermore, he understood that the logistically heavy Americans, with their need for substantial food, artillery and ammunition trains, were highly dependent on stable lines of communication. Hence he would not only ambush American columns, but he would also order bridges to be burnt, slowing down American response times to attacks elsewhere. On other occasions, he would launch raids on ill-protected civilian plantations, forcing the Americans to redeploy forces to tactically insignificant locations.

Eastern Indians, like all other Native Americans, placed a high value on personal bravery and the demonstration of the warrior spirit. Despite Osceola being the leader of the resistance, he obviously did not neglect these obligations. An official US report into the battle of Ouithlecoochee in 1836, in which Osceola personally led an ambush against an American column, pays

▲ An attack on Fort King by Native Americans under Osceola during the Seminole Wars, 1835. If the Indians couldn't take a main fortification, they would often set fire to outlying buildings.

genuine respect to the chief's martial bravery:

"Osceola was observed foremost of all his men in this battle, and was well known to General Clinch and many of his men. He wore a red belt, and three long feathers. Having taken his stand behind a tree, he would step boldly out, level his rifle, and bring down a man at every fire; nor was he dislodged until several volleys from whole platoons had been fired upon him. The tree behind which he stood was literally cut to pieces. It is almost a wonder that he had not now fulfilled the measure of his threat made on a former occasion, which was to kill General Clinch. He probably tried his best to do it, for the general received several shots through his clothes. General Thompson, Charles Omathla, and General Clinch were the three persons he had declared vengeance against."

This account bears testimony to the Indian skill with firearms, Osceola managing to "bring down a man with every fire." In doing so it illustrates the disparity between American and Indian fire tactics. From the Indian side, each man is taking individual aimed shots, and the threat against General Clinch indicates that officers were specific targets for the Indian marksmen. In contrast, the US soldiers are firing coordinated platoon volleys at single targets, a major waste of ammunition, especially against someone behind a tree, which would have been perfectly resistant to contemporary musket ball ammunition.

▼ Ambush - the shooting of General Braddock at Fort Duquesne, Pittsburgh, 1755. Note both the fast movement of the attackers between pieces of solid cover and the individualistic approach to selecting targets, officers being primary victims.

Raiding

The example of the Seminole Wars shows that the Eastern Indians were capable of sustained organized resistance, not just localized raiding, although the latter did form an important constant in the martial life of a tribe. One of the best descriptions of the distinction between raiding and outright war is from William Kessel and Robert Wooster's *Encyclopedia of Native American Wars & Warfare:*

"For the most part, raids were designed to search out and procure enemy property. Raiding expeditions were generally directed by an experienced leader and were formed by as few as five to 15 or more men. Traveling quietly they would locate an enemy and with as much stealth as possible take enemy possessions and occasionally enemy lives. Wars, on the other hand, involved much more organization and planning. An experienced war chief often led the expedition of many men. The primary purposes of wars were to avenge deaths and kill the enemy. Both raids and wars also provided opportunities for novices as well as experienced warriors to gain personal prestige."

– *Kessel and Wooster* (2005)

Raiding had various purposes, but as Kessel and Wooster here imply, the raid was primarily a short-term tactical action rather than part of a prolonged strategic campaign (although the raid could contribute to such a campaign). During a small-scale action against another tribe, the clash between rival warriors might take on an almost ritualistic feel. The two sides might face each other openly, firing the occasional arrow, exchanging insults or even compliments, then draw together in a group for a brief clash of arms, resulting in a few injuries or perhaps even a death or two among the combatants.

Yet the raid could take on considerable proportions of up to (although rarely) 1000 men or more, especially when it was directed at an enemy fort or village, and could have more serious consequences for one side or the other. Such a major expedition could take on a festive feel, with multiple groups of warriors joining loosely together to journey to the target.

▼ Native American warriors massacre a settler column, the close-quarters killing done with ball-and-spike war clubs. Such columns were extremely vulnerable to attack, as they invariably used well-worn trails that were prone to ambushes.

Attacking Fortifications

If facing a fortification, the attackers essentially had two options—direct or indirect assault, the latter often implying siege tactics. Some of the best explored examples of Indian versus Indian assaults relate to Iroquois attacks on Huron or French fortifications during the seventeenth century. For the direct assault, the Iroquois would literally run up to the outer defences of the fortification, moving as fast as possible to minimize exposure to enemy musketeers and bowmen firing from behind their barricades. While closing up to the fort, their own gunners and bowmen would lay down suppressing fire against the defenders, relying particularly on the shock value of their guns to intimidate the enemy. Note that the attackers initially would have approached the fortification by stealth. This was no reenactment of European medieval city assaults, when the defenders would have been aware of the clanking, noisy attackers well in advance of their arrival. The Iroquois are also recorded as using armor to protect themselves from projectile weapons as they closed up to the enemy defences. Thick, wooden hand-held shields were carried, dense enough to stop a musket ball, or several warriors carried a portable screen to protect them as they advanced.

Once the warriors arrived at the wall, they obviously had to gain access. There were two primary options. First, the attackers could set about the walls with their hatchets, cutting through the wooden defences to create a hole big enough to push warriors through. The second route into the fortification was by using scaling devices to climb over the tops of the walls. Scaling ladders were one option, these being light-framed ladders made from boughs lashed together with rawhide or similar materials.

▲ **This stylized nineteenth-century view of a Seminole attack on an American blockhouse deprives the Native American warriors of the rapid movement they employed in the attack. Note, however, the irregular pattern of Native American musketry; they indeed avoided the volley fire often used by the settler armies.**

The protective screen mentioned above might also be leaned against the defences, the warriors using it as a step to gain access. Any other means of getting in would be used—there are records of upturned canoes being used to give a step up into enemy forts.

Indirect Approach

A frontal assault of a fortified village or outpost could be costly in terms of casualties, particularly if the fortification was equipped with cannon (primarily in the case of American outposts), which made short work of the wooden shields and armor of the attackers. The indirect approach, therefore, could be the wiser but more time-consuming option. In some instances, the fortification was simply encircled and laid siege to. This had its risks and costs—the besieging group would have to spend time away from their tribal subsistence duties, and there was always the threat of attack from reinforcements. Yet the indirect assault method provided several other options. The attackers could conduct frequent but persistent small-scale raids against the fortification, steadily nibbling away at the defences and defenders until the habitation became unviable. Any unprotected buildings, or food supplies outside the habitation would be destroyed, or the attackers would target enemy foraging parties as they ventured out. Alternatively, the attackers might conduct an assault on a nearby but unprotected village, forcing the defenders of the fortified village to venture out to provide assistance, where they could be engaged in the open.

Fort Denonville

A classic example of the indirect assault approach is that of the Iroquois campaign against the French-occupied Fort Denonville in 1687–88. The Governor of New France, Jacques-Rene de Brisay, Marquis de Denonville, established the fort in 1687 as part of his campaign to oust the Iroquois from the Great Lakes, a campaign that did little more than incite the Indians to retaliate. Instead of attacking the fort, the Indians simply increased their hostile presence around the garrison, making it dangerous for those inside to venture out.

In effect, the garrison became besieged, a state of affairs made worse by the onset of winter and their distance from reinforcements and resupply from Montreal. The Iroquois imposed disease and starvation conditions on the French soldiers, keeping them trapped and without reinforcements until Denonville was forced to abandon the fort altogether. Such was the Iroquois threat that it would be more than three decades before the French were able to maintain a presence on the Niagara. Attacks on fortifications illustrate that the Indian "way of war" did in fact include major operations focused on strategic gain, and not just loose strategies of raiding.

Defeat From Victory

Pursuing Indians, often after they had retreated during an attack, also soaked up American energy and supplies, particularly on account of the endurance of which the Indians were capable. Compared to the European settlers, the Indians were incredibly light on their feet in terms of logistics. A European column, not being trained to live off the land, would rely heavily on cumbersome supply trains, winding arduously throughout the convoluted tracks that twisted through the Eastern woodlands.

The Indians, by contrast, could live off the land in which they had hunted from their earliest years. Furthermore, their nimbleness of foot and knowledge of the local terrain meant that they were not constrained to travel along familiar routes. Their dietary requirements would almost equate to starvation rations for most Europeans. The captive Mary Rowlandson, held prisoner by the Indians and whisked along with her family at a brisk pace, was startled to see the efficiency with which they could feed themselves in the most barren of landscapes. She admits to earlier prejudices.

> "IT WAS THOUGHT, IF THEIR CORN WERE CUT DOWN, THEY WOULD STARVE AND DIE WITH HUNGER; AND ALL THAT COULD BE FOUND WAS DESTROYED, AND THEY DRIVEN FROM THAT LITTLE THEY HAD IN STORE, INTO THE WOODS, IN THE MIDST OF WINTER; AND YET HOW TO ADMIRATION DID THE LORD PRESERVE THEM FOR HIS HOLY ENDS, AND THE DESTRUCTION OF MANY STILL AMONG THE ENGLISH!"
>
> – ROWLANDSON (1682)

Rowlandson acknowledges that contemporary wisdom taught that destroying an Indian tribe's central food resources would result in the death of a people. In a sense she is right—as we shall see, sustained community existence was threatened by the European encroachment into Indian food sources. Yet in terms of the warrior himself, on operations, this was far from the case. Rowlandson goes on to explain how the Indians sourced nutrition on their arduous journey:

"Their chief and commonest food was groundnuts, they eat also nuts and acorns, artichokes, lilly roots, ground beans, and several other weeds and roots that I know not. They would pick up old bones, and cut them in pieces at the joints, and if they were full of worms and maggots, they would scald them over the fire, to make the vermine come out, and then boil them, and drink up the liquor, and then beat the great ends of them in a mortar, and so eat them. They would eat horses guts, and ears, and all sorts of wild birds which they could

FORTIFICATION ASSAULT

Iroquois warriors are here seen executing an attack on an enemy tribe's fortified village. On the approach to the fortification walls, the warriors protect themselves from arrows and (to a degree) musket balls by using wooden shields, which could be both multi-person or individual varieties. Canoes used for deployment could also provide some cover and a stepping platform for ascending the walls. Other warriors hack open the walls with tomahawks, creating access or firing holes.

▲ **The death of Shawnee leader Tecumseh at the battle of the Thames in 1813. Note the way that the Native American on the left attacks the horse with his tomahawk; the Native Americans quickly realized that mounts could be more vulnerable than riders.**

catch: Also bear, venison, beavers, tortoise, frogs, squirrels, dogs, skunks, rattle-snakes: Yea the very bark of trees; besides all sorts of creatures, and provision which they plundered from the English; I can but stand in admiration to see the wonderful power of God, in providing for such a vast number of our enemies in the wilderness, where there was nothing to be seen, but from hand to mouth. Many times in the morning, the generality of them would eat up all they had, and yet have some farther supply against they wanted. But now our perverse and evil carriages in the sight of the Lord, have so offended him, that instead of turning his hand against them, the Lord feeds and nourishes them up to be a scourge to the whole land."

– *Rowlandson* (1682)

This is a natural point to return to the fact that although the Indians fought a good fight, it was not enough to retain their lands or, in many cases, survive. There are several important reasons why this is so. Partly, as has been suggested already, the American Indians were excellent at fighting local wars, or settling temporary tribal clashes, but their mindset was not the same as that of the Europeans, which by the late nineteenth century had a "total war" inflexion. Note the following comment in Paul Wellman's 1934 publication *The Indian Wars of the West*:

"The Indian [was thought] as less than human and worthy only of extermination. We did shoot down defenseless men, and women and children at places like Camp Grant, Sand Creek, and Wounded Knee. We did feed strychnine to red warriors. We did set whole villages of people out naked to freeze in the iron cold of Montana winters. And we did confine thousands in what amounted to concentration camps."

–*Wellman* (1934)

It is hard to imagine, even with the frequent brutality of Indian behavior towards their enemies, this perspective existing in a tribal context. Indians would go on to destroy and displace, but the enemy was frequently accorded a notional respect, and objectives of military action tended to be land and horses, not the destruction of an entire people. The Eastern or other Native American tribes also had military weaknesses when compared to the settler Americans. First, the Indians never manufactured firearms or gunpowder themselves. This left them at the mercy of supplies from the Europeans, which could be controlled according to government agendas. The rapacious Europeans would also take over prime hunting or agricultural land, forcing the tribe to move on or disperse. Finally, the Native Americans were never a united force against the Europeans, as the Civil War demonstrated. Various alliances came and went, leaving them prey to the Europeans who could eventually marshal huge military manpower and federal unity.

Civil War Service

The ability of the Native Americans to live off the land as Rowlandson describes was integral to their success in war. It was their very skills in tracking and survival that led to the recruitment of large numbers of Native Americans as scouts in the US military forces. During the Civil War of 1861–65, nearly 29,000 Native Americans served on the side of either the Confederacy or the Union. In this role, the Native Americans were hybrid soldiers, often donning official issue military dress but with recognizable Native American elements, such as wielding tomahawks and scalping knives alongside their rifles.

Most of the Eastern Native American tribes were participants in the conflict in one way or another, hardly surprising since the primary battlefields were in the Eastern territories of the United States. This in itself weakened the Native American grip over the territories, either through compromising themselves in disadvantageous treaties with the losing Confederate side, or through factionalism brought about by different positions on the conflict. The Cherokee, for example, were already divided into several factions by the time of the Civil War, with each having a different position on relations with the settlers. Having been promised national independence by the Confederacy, most of the Cherokee allied themselves with the South. While the war raged, the Cherokee proved to be excellent allies of the Confederacy, especially in conducting guerilla-style warfare. On September 19, 1864, for example, Cherokee troops of the Native American Cavalry Brigade (under the leadership of charismatic leader Stand Watie) inflicted 200 casualties on the Union at the Second Battle of Cabin Creek, also capturing 129 supply wagons, 740 mules and taking 120 prisoners.

▲ A studio portrait of Stand Watie (1806–71). A three-quarter Cherokee, he lead the tribe, who allied themselves with the Confederacy. At the end of the war he held the rank of brigadier-general in the Confederate Army.

A composite unit of Eastern tribes also formed Company K of the 1st Michigan Sharpshooters, earning distinction in famous battles such as Wilderness, Spotsylvania and Crater. Yet service in the Civil War proved to be a poisoned chalice for many Native American forces. For the Cherokee, for example, the war depleted their already dwindling population by 6000 men, and at the end of the war their support for the Confederacy earned them the distaste of the Federal Government, and later acts and treaties saw their land ownership effectively annulled.

Glossary

Anglicize To make something English in a linguistic or cultural sense.
antipathy Strong feelings against something.
auxiliary troops Supplemental troops.
battlement The portion of the wall covering the top of a fort's tower.
bayonet A blade that can be attached to the end of a musket; to stab someone with such a blade.
colonize To settle and take over a place where other people already reside.
confederacy An alliance.
disperse To separate by spreading out.
displace To separate a person from their usual environment by threatening or harming them or their means of survival until they leave.
dispossession To deprive a person of some possession.
disputed area A region that multiple sovereign powers claims as being under their control.
edifice A building or other structure of substantial size.
guerrilla warfare A type of warfare that relies on surprise attacks and harassment instead of traditional frontline formations.
haft A hilt; a weapon's handle.
hilt A haft; the handle of a weapon.
hostility The ill will that one group or person has toward another.
intermediary A mediator.
Iroquois Confederacy An alliance between Native American tribes consisting of the Mohawks, Oneidas, Onondagas, Cayugas, and the Senecas that began in 1142. In 1722, the Tuscaroras joined the others.
New Echota Treaty The 1835 treaty that wrested control of land in the northern portion of Georgia from Cherokee Indians in exchange for $5 million.
palisades Long, pointed stakes that are placed next to each other to form a defensive barrier.
rawhide A cow's skin.
scalping Cutting off the skin and hair on a portion of the crown of a person's head after killing them, as a trophy.
smock A garment worn over clothes.
Trail of Tears The forced removal of Cherokees from land in northern Georgia in 1838 after the 1835 signing of the New Echota Treaty.

Further Reading

Leahy, Todd, and Nathan Wilson. *Historical Dictionary of Native American Movements.* Lanham, MD: Rowman & Littlefield, 2016.

Lenik, Edward J. *Amulets, Effigies, Fetishes, and Charms: Native American Artifacts and Spirit Stones from the Northeast.* Tuscaloosa, AL: The University of Alabama Press, 2016.

Lobo, Susan, Steve Talbot, and Traci L. Morris. *Native American Voices: A Reader.* Abingdon, UK: Routledge, 2016.

Machajewski, Sarah. *The Cherokee People.* New York, NY: Gareth Stevens Publishing, 2015.

Madsen, Deborah L. *The Routledge Companion to Native American Literature.* Abingdon, UK: Routledge, 2016.

Martinez, Donna, Grace Sage, and Azusa Ono. *Urban American Indians: Reclaiming Native Space.* Santa Barbara, CA, and Denver, CO: Praeger, 2016.

McNab, Chris. *Native American Warriors: 1500 CE-1890 CE.* New York, NY: Chartwell Books, 2016.

Reséndez, Andrés. *The Other Slavery: The Uncovered Story of Indian Enslavement in America.* Boston, MA: Houghton Mifflin Harcourt, 2016.

Smithers, Gregory D. *The Cherokee Diaspora: An Indigenous History of Migration, Resettlement, and Identity.* New Haven, CT: Yale University Press, 2015.

Wakim Dennis, Yvonne, Arlene B. Hirschfelder, and Shannon Rothenberger Flynn. *Native American Almanac: More Than 50,000 Years of the Cultures and Histories of Indigenous Peoples.* Canton, MI: Visible Ink Press, 2016.

Websites

The Invasion of America: How the United States Took Over an Eighth of the World

http://invasionofamerica.ehistory.org

This interactive map offers users a look at the progression of colonialism and westward expansion through Native American territories.

Isuma TV
http://www.isuma.tv
This multimedia platform offers a space where indigenous peoples can create their own channel on which they share videos targeting their desired audience.

NativeWeb
https://www.nativeweb.org/resources/news_media_television_radio
The NativeWeb website has many links to various forms of media that cover contemporary Native Americans and other indigenous peoples.

Index